Hiking with Kids

*Taking those first steps
with young hikers*

Robin Tawney

FALCON®

HELENA, MONTANA

*A***FALCON**GUIDE®

Falcon® Publishing is continually expanding its list of recreational guidebooks. All books include detailed descriptions, accurate maps, and all the information necessary for enjoyable trips. You can order extra copies of this book and get information and prices for other Falcon® books by writing Falcon, P.O. Box 1718, Helena, MT 59624 or by calling toll-free 1-800-582-2665. Also, please ask for a copy of our current catalog. Visit our website at www.Falcon.com or contact us by e-mail at falcon@falcon.com.

Illustrations by Amy Kelley.
Cover photo by Larry Prosor.

Library of Congress Cataloging-in-Publication Data
Tawney, Robin, 1949–
    Hiking with Kids / by Robin Tawney.
      p.   cm. — (A FalconGuide)
    ISBN 1-56044-816-2
    1. Hiking for children. 2. Family recreation. I. Title. II. Falcon guide.
GV199.54 .T39 2000
796.51—dc2

                                                                99-056935

CAUTION

Outdoor recreational activities are by their very nature potentially hazardous. All participants in such activities must assume responsibility for their own actions and safety. The information contained in this guidebook cannot replace sound judgment and good decision-making skills, which help reduce exposure, nor does the scope of this book allow for the disclosure of all the potential hazards and risks involved in such activities.

Learn as much as possible about the outdoor recreational activities in which you participate, prepare for the unexpected, and be cautious. The reward will be a safer and more enjoyable experience.

For the Tawney Corps of Engineers—Land, Mikal,
and Whitney—and Amanda, Chris, Marci, Corey,
Kelsi, Michael Tee, Erin, Jackie, Ann, Charlie, Alpha,
Joe, Leah, Jenna, Brian, Megan, and kids of all ages

In memory of Jake, my four-footed muse
and constant companion

Contents

The bear went over the mountain,
The bear went over the mountain,
The bear went over the mountain,
And what do you think he saw?

He saw another mountain,
He saw another mountain,
He saw another mountain,
And what do you think he did?

He climbed that other mountain,
He climbed that other mountain,
He climbed that other mountain,
And what do you think he saw?

He saw another mountain,
He saw another mountain,
He saw another mountain,
And what do you think he did?

He climbed that other mountain,
He climbed that other mountain,
He climbed that other mountain,
And what do you think he saw?

Preface

I never had a stroller for my oldest children and, believe me, I never missed it. To me, loading the baby or toddler in a child carrier meant freedom. As we went about our downtown errands, I pitied the parents and nannies pushing cumbersome strollers, always on the lookout for sidewalk obstructions and incoming missiles—like stumbling pedestrians or red-hot cigarettes—that might strike their low-riding infants.

With a child on my back, running errands easily evolved into hiking whenever I needed to touch base with the natural world. At first, the kids were passive passengers: I went, so they went. Then hiking came naturally as each child became an able walker, eager to see everything up close and personal. In filling my own soul, I unwittingly had begun filling my childrens', as well.

Curiosity about the natural world still brings us all to our knees. As I write, my youngest—now a teenager—comes in from her chores with a beetle for me to inspect. We share our wonder at this marvel of nature and release it to its backyard habitat. Appreciation and stewardship are wonderful by-products of our time on the trail and the driving forces behind this book.

Special acknowledgment is due my chief fan and husband, William Nichols, for his patience and understanding; to my father Robert Brown for painstakingly proofing yet another manuscript; and to my mother Cidney Brown for allowing me, as a child, to clamber over wave-splashed boulders and to spend golden hours exploring in the outdoors.

Parents and children who provided grist for this book include Rae Dabbert, Jim Gouaux, Grant Parker, Jean and Chuck Parker, Charlie Stevenson, and countless families and hiking companions. I have learned much from you all. Lastly, I thank my children, Land, Mikal, and Whitney, for the hours they each spent with me in the child carrier and on terra firma.

Hiking in the Great Outdoors is a simple gift we all can give our children, grandchildren, and young friends. Unlike playing music, writing poetry, painting pictures, or other activities that also can fill your soul, hiking does not require any special skill. All you need to do is put one foot in front of the other in the outdoors, repeatedly. And breathe deeply.

Author's note: Grandparents and other significant adults, this book is written for you, as well as parents. Wherever you see the word "parent," just substitute "grandparent" or "grown-up friend." You, too, can enjoy hiking with kids!

1

Why Hike? Why Now? Why Not!

*The world is so full of a number of things,
I'm sure we should all be happy as kings.*
—Robert Louis Stevenson

Time management books line the shelves of libraries and bookstores, and form a tidy row along the edge of my desk. All purport to help adults eke efficiency and excellence from every minute of every day. Compartmentalizing, prioritizing, and strategic planning may work on the job, but try saying "Later!" to a tearful toddler or teen when family time isn't scheduled for another hour. The essence of parenting is "Now!"

Flexibility is the key. Even though our children lead increasingly structured lives—music and dance lessons, soccer practice—they are still kids. They need an abundance of time to play, to ramble, and to explore. And they need us.

Spending a day on the trail cuts right to the "Now!" by allowing parents to give children undivided attention, away from the hassles (and comforts) of daily life. Even if we walk the same path a million times, each outing presents a new opportunity to share spontaneous discoveries about the natural world and about each other. At the end of every day in the outdoors, we return home with a trove of new family stories.

Hiking with very young children puts them in touch with nature for the first time. Even the tiniest infants delight in the interplay of shadows, shapes, and colors as they peer out from the cozy security of their child carriers. Toddlers revel in testing new walking skills and in naming each new find along the trail. Preschoolers, with ever-increasing stamina, morph into aerobic naturalists, dashing up the trail, then screeching to a halt when they spy interesting bugs or trickling streams.

Hiking with elementary school children lays the groundwork for parent-child communication, step by step. Nature becomes a springboard for discussions about family values as youngsters learn to apply ethical behavior in an outdoor setting. Self-confidence and self-reliance naturally evolve as pre-adolescents hike farther and farther, all the while adding to their body of knowledge about the natural world.

Hiking can be a safety valve for teenagers, allowing precious time away from the critical eyes of peers or adults. A day on the trail provides teens and parents private time to talk about mundane or meaty matters, while delighting in the wonders of nature. We begin to let go and prove our trust when our teens take risks—like scrambling over rocks and fording icy streams. Taking responsibility for personal safety is an important step toward eventual independence.

Hiking is a gift we can give ourselves and our children. The cost is minimal, yet the experience is priceless and pays

Hiking is a gift we can give ourselves and our children.

dividends over a lifetime, as avid hikers can attest.

From childhood summers at an outdoor camp—savoring nature and sleeping under the stars at night—a senior hiker developed the concept that his own kids would be better people if they were out in nature. He stuck by that concept and now relates, "The nicest thing about spending time with my own children out-of-doors is that we all had a good time. It formed a lifelong bond and is a continual source of reminiscence."

A woman reflects on a lifetime of hiking with her father, her husband, her children, and her grandchildren: "Hiking does much more for the soul than it does for your body. I almost never go out, even on daily walks with my dog, without thinking I am the luckiest person in the world."

* * *

Still need a reason to hike with your kids? How about this one: a day spent exercising in the fresh air will help you all sleep better!

2

Preparation: All Together Now

Red skies in the morning, sailors take warning.
Red skies at night, sailors' delight.

Setting adult goals and expectations for any hike with kids is an instant recipe for disaster. Your trip will be cooked the first time your youngster squats in the middle of the trail to examine a bug. One way or another, our children tell us— force us—to slow down and literally stop and smell the roses.

Think of hiking with kids as an ongoing adventure: each stage of your child's development provides new perspectives as you explore the natural world together. Only when your child is a portable infant can you set your own pace and choose your own trail.

If you start carrying your baby in a child carrier when he/she is quite small, carrying a squirming 25-pound toddler won't seem so bad later on. Begin with trips around town, so that you become accustomed to baby's weight, and baby gets used to extended periods in the carrier. Most infants readily adapt to the snuggly confines and fall asleep to the rhythm of your walk. Remember to stop periodically and unload baby for a wiggle break. Even tiny muscles can cramp.

Older babies riding high in back carriers enjoy eye contact with adults as they move down the trail. Use a hand mirror as a rear-view mirror, so baby can periodically see your face and you, in turn, can check on your tiny passenger.

As babies move toward toddlerhood, they revel in standing and jumping on the pack frame or kickstand, making you feel like a human pogo stick. Offer a diversion to these toddler antics: clip toys and teething rings to the pack frame, and pass back crackers for munching, if you don't mind a few crumbs on your neck.

Keep a fussy toddler entertained.

Once your little one starts to walk, you can still hike at your own speed, but only when he/she is fast asleep in the child carrier. During wakeful times, you will begin to hear "Down!", a powerful word in the new toddler vocabulary. Soon, "Down, down, down!" becomes a chant, increasing in volume with each step you take. Your toddler's vocals usually are accompanied by hair-pulling (yours) and lurching as he/she tries to bail out of the child carrier (one good reason for seat belts).

There is no reasoning with a toddler, so grant his/her fondest wish at the nearest safe spot on the trail. Every rock, every bug, and every berry vies for your toddler's attention and, thus, yours. A word of caution: some children will put everything they pick up into their mouths. Oral children need extra-vigilant parents to keep them from choking on stones and snacking on poisonous plants.

Very young children may soon tire of careening over uneven ground and may willingly settle into the child carrier. Others may insist on their own form of snail locomotion. If the latter is the case, make a quick transition to the slow mode. Today's hike may just be a couple of hundred yards, but both you and your toddler will become familiar with every square inch of the terrain. Plan to be on the trail (literally) for just a couple of hours.

At this point, you may decide "hiking" is not worth the two-hour drive to a trailhead and settle for a walk around your neighborhood, or you may want to capitalize on your toddler's "natural" interest and choose a trail closer to home.

With time and patience, you can gradually increase your distance.

As your kids become more capable walkers, choose short flat hikes that lead to a destination where there is a guarantee of action. A sure bet is slow-moving water for wading, swimming, fishing, or skipping rocks. (Don't forget to bring along water shoes or old tennies; hiking in wet shoes is definitely not fun.) Older children relish the challenge of reaching a mountain summit. If the mountain sports a fire lookout or a snowfield, all the better. Just don't make any promises you can't fulfill, like, "Of course we'll see mountain goats when we get to the summit."

Follow these simple steps to help make the hike an activity the entire family will enjoy:

Choose a place to hike

To find a suitable trail—fairly flat without obvious hazards like a raging river or a lake with precipitous banks. Talk to other parents who hike, or go somewhere you have hiked before. Other likely sources of information include local nature centers, outdoor equipment stores, and chambers of commerce. Load up on maps and information for trails on public land by visiting state forest and parks departments, or federal agencies such as the USDA Forest Service, Bureau of Land Management, and National Park Service. Area guidebooks often highlight popular hikes for a variety of abilities.

Even if you are not a joiner, membership in an outdoor club may be worthwhile. Local clubs, or state or national organizations with local chapters organize hikes for novices, as well as experts. Hiking with people who are familiar with an area adds a new dimension to your experience.

Consult a topographic map of the area where you plan to hike before you set foot on the trail. A topo, unlike other maps, has contour lines that show elevation above sea level and help interpret landforms. Study the trail you have chosen and see how steep or flat the land really is. Whenever possible, choose a circular route; it will be far more interesting than hiking both ways on the same trail.

Planning hikes becomes a family affair as your children get older. Poring over topo maps together teaches kids to "read" the lay of the land, a survival skill that may someday come in handy. Find your destination on the map and follow the trails that will take you there. Then as you hike, consult the map periodically to see how far you've come.

If you are unsure about the suitability of a trail for family hiking, pre-hike it with other adults.

Consider the season

Trails may be muddy or snow-covered in early spring or late fall. Find out which trails are in the open and more likely to be dry than others that meander through thick forests. In summer, a tree-lined trail provides welcome shade, and a shallow creek running alongside the trail is a happy bonus.

Keep away from areas where bears are emerging from their winter's sleep, or other animals may be tending newborns. Sometimes such areas are officially closed; other times we humans must rely on our common sense to stay away.

Choose a hike that involves as little driving as possible
Curvy roads can upset stomachs, and stuffy vehicles can leave the entire family feeling fuzzy-headed. Sitting for hours in the same position may cramp muscles needed for hiking.

Hope for the best and plan for the worst
Planning ahead can help prevent catastrophes on the trail.
- Check on trail and weather conditions before leaving home.
- Leave a trip plan with someone who will alert authorities if you do not return as scheduled.
- Scale the length and duration of hikes to the capability and interest of your youngest child. Plan to walk at his/her speed, and double the amount of time you estimate it will take to get to your destination. If you are carrying an infant or toddler, know your own limitations, too; you don't want to collapse from exhaustion on the trail. Allow even more time for rugged or steep terrain.
- Use liberal amounts of sunscreen and bug repellent before you begin walking and apply more periodically throughout your hike.
- Keep well hydrated; carry at least one liter of water per person.
- Make sure everyone has adequate gear for a day afield. (See appendix.)
- Think about and be prepared to handle potential emergencies along the trail.

Take lots of pictures

Preparation is an important part of recreation. After preparation comes action, then reflection. That is where cameras come in.

Remember, this is a family hike, not a forced march

Climb peaks you want to climb and hike trails you want to hike with your spouse, partner, or friends. When you are with your kids, be with your kids.

One parent describes his family's first hike this way: "When my three kids were between ages 5 and 9, we hiked up Bass Creek. I had never gone there without getting to the lake and beyond (at least 8 miles), but the kids got tired and they ate snacks, chased frogs, built dams in the side creeks. They were happy.

*You never know what kind of critters
you'll meet on the trail.*

"Each time we stopped, I looked at my watch. The light faded, and we hiked back down the trail. We never reached my goal, but for the kids, the main reason for going hiking was to have fun. And they did."

Fortunately, this dad recognized the conflict between his expectations and his kids'. A couple of summers later, his patience was rewarded: "The kids set the goals. They would see a peak and say, 'Let's go!'"

TOOLS FOR THE TRAIL

Fortunately, hiking is not equipment-intensive and does not require a huge outlay of cash. It takes only a few items to make hiking with children a comfortable and fun-filled experience. A list of those bare necessities appears below. Buying equipment on sale, off-season, or secondhand makes this family pursuit even more affordable.

A word of caution: don't waste your money on military surplus gear. Most of it is heavy and cumbersome. After one hike with army leftovers, you probably would rush to replace them with lightweight, waterproof, and durable packs, ponchos, and tents.

Child carriers

I learned early on that comfort is essential for baby *and* me. For baby, comfort means a cozy, padded nest securely fastened to a parent. For me, comfort means a pack that distributes the baby's or toddler's weight as evenly as possible to eliminate my own shoulder and back strain.

Carrying an infant kangaroo-style in a soft front pack provides snug security and hands-free hiking. To haul babies from birth to 25 pounds, select a wraparound carrier that cradles your infant, provides him/her with head and lumbar support, and has leg openings wide enough to prevent chafing and loss of circulation.

The front carrier's suspension system should include a padded adult harness and hip belt to stabilize your load and protect your lower back. The carrier's design should be uncomplicated so that you can load and unload your growing infant without assistance. Options may include permanent or removable pockets for stowing extra diapers and a hood to protect baby from sun and rain.

Once your baby can sit without support, he/she can move to your back. Since you will use a back carrier until your tiny hiker is a capable walker, go for all the bells and whistles you can afford. Your investment will be returned by many happy hours and miles on the trail.

A sturdy aluminum frame, like that of a conventional backpack, supports this type of child carrier. At the base of the pack frame, a padded hip belt helps stabilize the load and allows you to shift the pack's weight for maximum comfort. A foam-filled lumbar pad and a cushioned back panel of mesh fabric add support and ventilation. Each component of the suspension system should be fully adjustable to custom-fit adults of varying torso lengths.

The baby's cockpit should include padded side panels and a padded sling seat with wide leg openings, all fully adjustable to accommodate a growing child. The top of the pack frame should be thickly padded, as well, because that is where baby will inevitably rest a sleepy head.

Most importantly, make sure your little one is secured by a shoulder harness with a foam-filled chest pad and a quick-release seat belt with crotch strap. Properly harnessed and belted, your child won't be forcefully ejected if you should stumble. Seat belts save lives on the trail, as well as on the highway.

For safety in loading and unloading, the carrier also should have a hinged kickstand with a wide tripod base. *Never, never, never* use the kickstand to create a stand-alone chair. Kids squirm and accidents happen. The child *carrier* is to be *carried*.

Virtually every child carrier features a zippered compartment beneath the sling seat for stowing extra diapers and clothing. Some carriers also have external pockets, an automatically retractable kickstand, rubber stabilizing feet, or safety reflectors. Detachable options may include a soft lining for the cockpit, gear bags (like a daypack or diaper duffel), or a canopy to block sun and rain. These extras can nearly double the basic pack weight from 4.75 pounds to 9.5 pounds, a significant addition considering the maximum load of most child carriers—60 pounds or a 35-pound child plus gear. Choose only the options you think you will need.

Daypacks

There comes a time when all toddlers have had it with being confined to child carriers and want "OUT!" When that happens, hand your child a child-sized daypack to carry.

Size is important here. Make sure that first daypack fits comfortably, with shoulder straps that won't slip off narrow toddler shoulders. If you give your toddler an adult-sized pack "to grow into," you inevitably will end up carrying it *and* your own daypack on the trail. My kids' first daypack (passed down as the kids grew) could stow a raincoat or lunch, but not both. For an older child, the pack that carries books on school days can double as a daypack on weekends.

Your daypack should be big enough to haul the family first aid and emergency kits, trail food, an extra water bottle or two, your personal gear, and anything the kids can't carry. Lots of options are available.

Footwear

Parents need sturdy shoes to lug a child or the bulk of the family's supplies. Today's lightweight hiking boots provide stabilizing support, traction, and ankle protection—features that become absolutely essential as load and distance increase. For the kids? Comfy, well broken-in tennies with traction soles will do just fine for beginners, but as your child spends more time actually hiking, he/she will eventually want and need sturdier footwear.

When selecting those first honest-to-goodness hiking boots, make sure you both try on several pairs. Five-pound leather boots may look great in the store, but how will they feel after several hours on the trail? Modern boot technology provides us with a variety of lightweight materials that are breathable, durable, and waterproof or water-resistant in an assortment of styles and prices, all for less than 1 pound for kids, or less than 2 pounds to 4.5 pounds for adults. Why suffer?

Clothing

Whatever the season, always hope for the best and prepare for the worst by carrying appropriate clothing for *any* weather condition you might encounter. In the outdoors, the layered look is in! Make sure that all your layers of clothing fit loosely to allow an insulating layer of air to lie between them. When clothing is snug, moisture from perspiration will condense, and you will feel clammy cold or steamy hot, depending on the air temperature and the level of your exertion.

As far as fabrics go, the outdoors is not the place to go natural. Cotton and wool are fine for town, but if they get wet—from rain, snow, or perspiration—they stay wet. Blue jeans are especially uncomfortable when wet; they cling to your legs and take forever to dry out. Choose synthetic wicking fabrics and quick-drying polar fleece and nylon instead of natural fibers. You will be glad you did.

Hats are a must. Fifty percent or more of the body's radiant heat escapes through the head. When the temperature drops, cap that heat loss with a cozy knit or polar fleece hat. With your head covered, you will find your hands and feet stay warmer, too. In summer, a lightweight billed hat will allow excess body heat to escape while deflecting the sun's toasty rays. Caps with bills and flaps that cover the backs of necks are especially nice for infants and toddlers riding in child carriers.

Since I live in mountainous country, I always carry hats for sun and warmth, even in the summer. I also bring along gloves or mittens, a long-sleeved shirt, and a hooded raincoat or poncho that doubles as a windbreaker. For the bottom half, I pack long pants (if I'm wearing shorts); rainpants to keep me dry and provide a buffer from the wind; and an extra pair of socks in case my feet get wet. Usually these extras never leave my pack, but once in a while, they mean the difference between comfort and misery.

In the "bridge" seasons of spring and fall, I add a polar fleece sweater or sweatshirt and an insulating vest; long underwear bottoms layer easily under my other pants.

Sporting goods stores and mail-order catalogs offer mini-sized versions of adult outdoor gear and clothing. If you dress your hiking children like you dress yourself, you can gauge their comfort level by your own. Keep in mind that the baby passively hitching a ride on your back is not expending much energy, so dress him/her accordingly.

Other essentials

Every hiker should carry at least a sweatshirt (preferably polar fleece) and a pocket-sized space blanket; rainwear or a big

garbage bag to substitute; a whistle (to signal for help if sep-
arated from the group); a water bottle (at least one liter per
person); a bandanna (to use as a sunshade, ear muffs, washcloth, towel, or sling); a small flashlight with extra batteries
(in case you get caught in the dark); and a sacred, high-
energy candy bar (to be used only in an emergency).

On family hikes, distribute among the adults: first-aid
and emergency kits; insect repellent and sunscreen; map and
compass (you can substitute a global positioning system for
the compass, but be aware that a GPS might not work
in mountainous country); knife; toilet paper and plastic
trowel (for bathroom needs); trail food; and plastic bags for
litter.

If you are hiking in snake country, add a snakebite kit.
If you are hiking in bear country, each adult should carry a
large and easily accessible canister of pepper spray. You can
dangle bells from your pack to warn the bruins of your presence, or you can do as my family does: make noise.

Extras

Tuck a cheap folding umbrella into an easily accessible pocket
of your pack. An umbrella may look silly on the trail, but it
will help keep you, baby, and your gear dry in a sudden
downpour.

Telescopic hiking poles add stability and safety on wet,
slippery trails, or when carrying a child carrier or heavy pack
on uneven terrain. Use a pair to reduce stress to your knees
and lower back and to help you maintain an upright posture.

Keep a camera handy in a belt pouch or fanny pack worn in reverse. That way, you will always be ready for that perfect photo-op.

You can never carry too many snacks on a family outing. According to one parent, "Carrying extra food and drink is not nearly as much trouble as carrying too little food and drink."

A list of items for your first-aid and emergency kits appears in Appendix I. Appendix II includes a checklist of essentials and more ideas for items you may want to carry with you.

* * *

Anyone who has hiked behind someone lugging a child with a dirty diaper can tell you the secret of hiking with kids is that old Scout motto: "Be Prepared." Make a list and check it twice. If you are hiking with babies, be sure to bring more than enough diapers!

Personally, I continue to stick with my own, time-tested maxim: If you don't think you'll need something, you will; take it along and you won't—or you just might.

LOST AND FOUND

All hikers need to know how to stay found. Teach your kids some simple rules and help them develop good old-fashioned common sense.

- No one (including adults) should hike alone. Each year, solo hikers make headlines when they run into serious trouble without a companion to administer first-aid or go for help. Even families should use the buddy system so that older children, frustrated by their siblings' poky pace, don't strike out on their own.

- Have your older children help plan your family's hike so they understand where they are going and how long they will be gone.
- Smart hikers wear brightly colored clothing that can be easily spotted in an outdoor setting. Stay away from camouflage and earth tones. Green, brown, tan, and gray blend with natural surroundings.
- Every hiker should wear or carry a whistle to use only if he/she is in danger or cannot locate the family group. A blast of three short "tweets," the universal distress call, carries farther than the human voice and will tell rescuers (family or not) where to find a missing person. Repeat the trio of loud bursts until help arrives. I learned the value of whistle communication in the wild at Disney World, when a friend's 6-year-old disappeared into the crowd. After a few anxious moments for everyone, the child blew her emergency whistle and was quickly reunited with her parent.
- The command to "sit and stay" is not just for dogs. Someone who is lost should stop walking the minute he/she realizes it and *stay put*. The lost person should remain calm and think about when he/she last saw the family, then blow the whistle. Those searching can whistle in response to reassure the missing one that help is on its way.

WEATHER OR NOT

Unless the weather forecast is especially grim, don't let it spoil your plans. Remember, meteorologists give themselves (and you) a percentage of error, and you might just miss a spectacular day in the outdoors. Besides, the nature of

Even a bad-weather day can be good.

weather is change, and if the heavens do open up, you are bound to come home with a story to tell.

Watch the sky for puffy cumulus clouds. If these cottonball clouds are small, you can predict a nice day with a chance of scattered showers. If the puffs combine into larger clouds and turn dark, get ready for rain, lightning, and possibly hail.

Make sure your rainwear is at the top of your pack where you can grab it when you feel a sprinkle. Buffered against the elements and still hiking or hunkered together under a makeshift shelter, turn your attention (and your kids') to meaty topics, like how rain and wind affect wild animals, how Native Americans and pioneers coped with weather, how rain feels and smells. Turn precipitation into a positive; it can't last forever.

"The best times outdoors have been in bad weather," says one seasoned hiker and grandmother. "I remember coming out on the trail from Sperry Chalet over Gunsight Pass (in Glacier National Park). It began pouring rain as we hiked along the river bottom. I told stories. The sun came out when we reached the top and the end of the trail, and we did a little sun dance. We crowded into our little Honda Civic and shared the wonderful feeling of having survived."

The kids will be watching you closely to see how you respond to any change in the weather. When adults keep the mood light, even a bad-weather day can be good. Being caught in a torrential rain is no big deal if you don't make it one. Just be prepared!

If you wait for a perfect day, you will rarely go anywhere, and you will never share stories of "How We Survived.'

A caveat

The rules change when you hike with an infant or toddler. Stay home when it looks like a storm is brewing. If you are already on the trail when the temperature drops and the rain starts to fall, make sure baby is dressed appropriately and stays dry. Otherwise, he/she could become hypothermic—a major medical calamity.

3

Happy Trails:
Tips for Maintaining Forward Motion and a Positive Attitude

A big turtle sat on the end of a log,
Watching a tadpole turn into a frog.

If you've followed the advice in the previous chapter, your entire brood is properly dressed for the weather, slathered with sunscreen and bug repellent, well hydrated, and ready for any emergency. At first the kids bounce down the trail, anxious to explore unfamiliar territory. A while later, the newness wears thin. Your junior hikers progressively tire of walking through a heavy forest or climbing a steep and rocky slope. The goal they set for today's hike seems a long way off.

How can you avoid a sit-down strike?

First, take a break and drink some water. Second, think about your children and their abilities. (Is this slow-down for real? Are you tired, too?) Third, if you know the kids still have energy to burn, gently remind them about what's up ahead and how anxious you are to reach that goal, too. Don't nag or push too hard. Nagging only results in creating sullen prisoners on a forced march.

Remember that you are on the trail to have fun. Do what you can to sustain a happy hiking mood. Here are a few suggestions:

- Do some homework ahead of time. Share what you have learned about the natural and human history of the area before you get to the trailhead and as you hike. Then look for evidence of this history, like signs of a glacier that covered this very trail 2 million years ago, or the lava ejected from a long-ago volcano. If Native Americans hunted in these parts, imagine what it was like to live off the land with only Stone Age tools.
- Try to visualize what this area looks like in winter. Would you be able to find the trail if it was snow-covered?
- Make up stories as you hike. Start with something you all see, like a cloud, or a chipmunk skittering across the trail, and spin a tale from there. Take turns embellishing the story. A good story can take you a long way up the trail as everyone listens intently to the twisting plot and eagerly waits to add to it.
- Sing songs. Let your kids lead you in song or teach them some oldies-but-goodies.
- Count anything. If there is more than one of something, you can count it. Count the number of bird or flower species you see; if you see a lot of one kind, count the individuals. Count the number of steps to the top of the hill.
- Play games like "I am thinking of ..." or "I spy... ." One person sees something along the trail and describes it with-

out divulging what it really is, while the rest of the family tries to guess what he/she sees. Focus on natural subjects, and the entire family will marvel at each other's observations. In a variation called "20 Questions," the family learns clues only by asking questions. In either case, make sure you take turns.

- Sometimes it is hard to hear each other when the path is narrow and the family walks single-file, so walk in silence, pretending you are an animal and this is your habitat. Quietly walk toe to heel like animals do, and listen carefully to all the sounds around you by cupping both ears forward with your hands. Your hands help magnify sound, like the large ears of a deer or moose. Are you predator or prey? How would you move through this area? Where would you live? Walking quietly also is a good way to relax and think deep thoughts—shallow ones.

- Take frequent short breaks for sips of water. Hydration is important to keep bodies performing at their best. When you stop, make sure everyone rests standing up. Horses do it. If you sit down, your muscles may tense and make hiking much harder after your break. Make sure everyone has a supply of lemon drops or other hard fruity candies to stave off thirst between stops.

- While you are resting, pull out a pair of binoculars or a spotting scope, and scan the places where forest and meadow meet for signs of wildlife. If the woods are thick, be still and listen for birds, bugs, and small mammals. Tiny mud chimneys along a creek or lake bank may mean

*Baby in front and a daypack in back
make for a balanced load.*

you have found crayfish condos. You don't have to be an
expert to spot wildlife. Just use your good senses!

- Stop to browse on wild berries (be sure you can identify
  the non-poisonous ones).
- Fresh air and exercise make everybody hungry. Keep food
  simple, healthy, and easy to pack or fix. Don't take food

that will spoil or melt. Recipes for and lists of some trail foods appear in Appendix IV.

- Some families enjoy hiking with other families with similar-aged kids or allow their own kids to take along friends. Either strategy works if all parties are game, but one whiner can drag down the whole group. Make sure you have a match when you add a hiking buddy.

- If you carry an infant in a front-load child carrier, you can haul a daypack, too. Wearing two packs front and back, like a sandwich board, balances your overall load and relieves your adult hiking companions from hauling your personal gear as well as their own.

- As your kids become capable hikers, give them a chance to clamber over boulders, cross scree fields, or perch on the edge of a cliff. Talk about the risks involved, then stand back and let them go. Allowing your offspring to "cut loose" responsibly boosts their confidence and self-esteem, and shows your trust in their growing capabilities.

- Celebrate when you reach your goal. Pull out the camera and a special treat you have saved for this moment. Be sure to catch your kids in front of a backdrop that shows their accomplishment—at the top of a craggy peak with a view of the valley below, with a fish freshly caught in a mountain stream, or on a rock in the middle of a gentle waterfall. Memories prompted by happy photos last a lifetime.

LION LEERY, BEAR AWARE

The chance of a brush with one of nature's major predators is practically nil, but it doesn't hurt to be prepared, just the same. When you and your kids know how to react in an encounter, you will all hike with more confidence and less fear about what lurks around the next bend.

Both bears and lions instinctively chase things that run away from them, and they move at lightning speed. You can never outrun them. To avoid a tragedy, stay cool and use your head.

Make sure your children understand that the action you take when you meet a mountain lion is different from what you do when you see a bear. How you respond could be a matter of life and severe mauling or death.

Mountain lions

Cougars, or mountain lions, eat meat. Some biologists theorize that they don't distinguish between people and deer, so children and small adults are potentially fair game.

In many parts of the country, the mountain lion population has ballooned in recent years, keeping pace with the ever-increasing number of deer. As urban development encroaches upon traditional habitat, deer migrate to the safety and bounty of no-hunting zones. Predators follow prey, increasing the odds of a confrontation between mountain lions and humans.

If you live in an area where the urban edge is blurred and deer are regularly seen in gardens, make sure you and your children know what to do if a lion appears in your backyard or on the trail:

- Get small children off the ground immediately.
- Do not run, and do not turn your back on the lion.
- Do not crouch or play dead. Try to make yourself as big and as threatening as possible by holding something over your head or by opening your jacket to make yourself appear broader.
- Stand your ground, speak firmly and constantly. You want to convince the lion that you are not prey and, in fact, that you may be a danger.
- Stay calm and move slowly. Back away slowly, facing the animal and throwing stones or poking sticks at it.
- If the lion attacks, fight back. Hit the animal in the head, and try to stay on your feet.

Bears

Unlike mountain lions, bears go out of their way to avoid humans. As far as diet goes, they are opportunists.

Bears almost always go for the easiest available meal—whether it falls in the meat or vegetable group—and they usually stay close to a good food source. They emerge from winter hibernation in early spring to frequent stream bottoms where they savor the spring green-up and dine on carcasses left by other predators. As spring stretches into summer, bears broaden their diets by feasting on grubs and insects. Late summer and fall find bears moving to berry patches and groves of whitebark pine.

Homo sapiens is rarely on the menu. Bears only attack people if they are startled or are trying to protect their cubs. If you make enough noise by talking, whistling, or swinging bells from your pack, bears usually retreat to cover rather than confront you.

If you meet a bear on the trail, be quiet. Hysterical screams will convince this near-sighted predator that you are a prey animal. Loud and assertive talk may be perceived as a threat.

Each hiking adult should carry bear pepper spray and know how and when to use it. According to research, most bear encounters occur when people and bears are within 100 feet of each other. If a bear approaches to within 30 or 40 feet, give it a blast of pepper spray. The sound and sight of the cloud of spray may be sufficient to scare the bear away, but if the bear charges, spray it directly in the face and repeat, if necessary.

Your protection depends on buying, carrying, and using the right pepper spray. The Interagency Grizzly Bear Committee (IGBC) recommends that you purchase only products clearly labeled "for deterring attacks by bears" and approved by the U.S. Environmental Protection Agency. Mace just won't do.

The spray should contain 1.4 percent to 1.8 percent capsaicin and related capsaicinoids (i.e., oleoresin capsicum) and be released in a shotgun-cloud pattern, not in a stream, at a minimum range of 25 feet. The cloud should linger at least 6 seconds.

Make your presence known when hiking in bear country.

To make sure you have enough spray for multiple blasts, the IGBC recommends that you carry a canister showing a net weight of at least 7.9 ounces, or 225 grams. A bear may not stop charging after just one blast. The amount of spray becomes even more important on windy, rainy, or cold days, or when encountering a highly protective sow or a bear with a fresh kill.

If, for some reason, you are caught off-guard, play dead. Fall face down, curl up in a ball, and lock your hands behind your head, keeping your arms as close to your body as possible. This modified fetal position protects vital organs, face, and neck. No matter what, try not to make any noise; screaming and fighting will only make the bear more aggressive. The bear may give up when it no longer senses danger. Even if you are injured, do not move for a while. If the bear returns and sees you move, it may resume its attack.

* * *

Unless a sign at the trailhead warns you to stay away, don't use the possibility of seeing a bear or a mountain lion as an excuse to stay home. Follow the tips outlined previously, and use your good common sense.

DON'T DRINK THE WATER

That clear rushing stream looks inviting, but before you slurp its icy water, consider this: just like your computer, this stream could have a bug.

In a week or two you may be wracked with cramping, foul-smelling diarrhea, abdominal distention, flatulence, nausea, vomiting, appetite loss, headaches, and low-grade fevers. These symptoms may last from one to three weeks, or years if they become chronic or relapsing. Is one sip worth this much suffering?

One of the many waterborne diseases that bring such discomfort is called giardiasis, and the parasite that causes it is *Giardia lamblia*. According to the federal Centers for Disease Control in Atlanta, no surface water in the world can be guaranteed free of these nasty microscopic cysts.

Giardiasis is spread through fecal-oral transmission, whereby some form of the cysts is shed in feces and enters a new host or victim by way of the mouth (read: sampling "pristine" waters). Animals or humans may deposit *Giardia* directly into a stream, river, pond, or lake, or nearby where the wee beasties are flushed into the water by runoff, rising water levels, or erosion. *Giardia* also may make their way to water on the feet of humans or animals or on the pelts of animals who roll in feces. Feces continually recontaminate remote watersheds where hardy parasites remain viable for months, particularly in cold water.

Giardiasis is not easily eradicated, either in the wilds or in the human body. While giardiasis is not fatal, it can be unpleasant and debilitating, and can occur without symptoms. An unaffected carrier could innocently contribute to the disease cycle by improperly disposing of his/her own feces.

No matter where you hike, the best defense against disease is to carry water from home. If you must use water from a natural source, purify it. You can use a commercial water filter/purifier (many lightweight models are available), or you can use iodine tablets. Be sure to follow manufacturer's instructions when using water purifiers or iodine tablets.

4

Trail Etiquette:
Civilized Behavior
Beyond Civilization

One, two, three, four, five,
I caught a fish alive.
Six, seven, eight, nine, ten,
I let him go again.

The Great Outdoors gives us all a sense of unbridled freedom. Out of sight and earshot of other humans, we can do as we please—within reason. Any civics teacher will tell you that responsibility goes hand-in-hand with freedom.

The National Wildlife Federation (NWF) identifies a global set of outdoor ethics that combines citizenship with the Golden Rule. The NWF list includes courtesy and consideration, respect, responsibility and accountability, compassion, integrity, fairness and justice, restraint, humaneness, selflessness, and common sense.

Get ready for a test on outdoor ethics whenever you hit the trail. Your family will encounter any number of dilemmas, from deciding what to do when you find a baby bird that has fallen from its nest to choosing the right location for a latrine. Some of the solutions to these questions may be black and white, while others seem maddeningly gray.

In every instance, your offspring will look to you for answers. Children naturally mimic adult behavior, and they are keenly aware when adults say one thing and do another. Quiet and consistent modeling speaks volumes. Excessive lecturing and moralizing probably will have the opposite effect on kids in the outdoors, just like it does at home.

Some basic guidelines for civilized behavior beyond civilization:

Follow the rules

Some rules are written down. Every national park and many other public parks, state and national forests, and wildlife refuges prohibit the possession, removal, or destruction of any plant, mineral, or animal. So, if the sign says, "No," don't pick the flowers, pocket the rocks, or carry off dropped antlers. If we bend or break the rules ("just this one little flower"), we teach our children to do the same. Following rules to the letter, no matter where we are, promotes good citizenship in our children.

If you pack it in, pack it out.

In the Great Outdoors, my family relishes the fact that cookie crumbs and sloshed drinks never need to be swept or sopped up. After all, Mother Nature will send in her clean-up crew of ants and other critters to take care of our messes. This is true only to a point. Crumbs and drips are one thing; candy wrappers and banana peels are another. The best rule of thumb is to treat the outdoors like your home and pick up after yourselves.

Hang a small plastic sack from your belt or pack, and encourage your offspring to pick up any litter they find. When you come upon a trashy campsite, take time to clean it up. Ask your kids what this mess says about the people who made it, and how the objects you find might injure wildlife. Impress on your children that being carefree and "letting George do it" doesn't work at home or in the woods.

When you pay attention to the result of thoughtless behavior and handle it according to your highest sense of right, your kids will recognize that littering is serious business.

Stay on the trail

When the trail is long and steep, and you know your destination is straight up there somewhere, resist the temptation to take a shortcut. That zigzag trail gradually ascending the steep mountain slope is designed to be slow and steady, but, more importantly, to minimize erosion. A beaten path straight up the hillside provides an instant channel for storm runoff, which eventually will wash out the very trail you are supposed to be using.

Other trails are cleared through fragile or sensitive areas to minimize visitor impact or to keep people away from areas where wildlife may be breeding or raising their young. Ask your kids why it is important to avoid trampling fragile habitat or disturbing animals. One set of footprints might not make a difference, but what if *everybody* left the trail?

Remember that you are a visitor

The trail that you wander so carefree leads through someone else's living room. Be aware of how your very presence affects the critters who live there. Leave portable radios and other personal electronic equipment at home. Unless you are hiking in bear country, ask your children to speak in conversational tones and save those shouts as calls of distress. Some animals will move at the slightest disturbance; others will hold their ground if they do not feel threatened.

Wildlife can be potentially dangerous. Most animals will go out of their way to avoid you, but if you surprise them or try to get a closer look, they may take defensive action. Approaching young animals is an especially risky business. Many animal mothers see humans as a threat and will defend their young against intrusion, no matter how innocent the intent. Others, like birds, will abandon their babies if they catch even a whiff of human scent on their young or in their nests.

Use binoculars, a spotting scope, or a telephoto lens to ensure safe wildlife viewing. If you are hiking with pets, know where they are at all times and keep leashes handy. You don't want Rover to flush a bear.

Don't feed the animals

They get all the nourishment they need naturally. When wild animals become dependent on human food, they become aggressive toward humans. A marmot or a tiny chipmunk begging to share your lunch might just mistake your finger for a carrot.

Respect landowner rights, and ask before hiking on private land

You wouldn't want hikers barging through your yard, trampling your shrubs and flowers, and scaring your pets. Well, neither do farmers and ranchers. Yet each year, unthinking people trespass on private land, leaving gates and fences agape. Livestock escape and landowners are forced to spend long hours undoing what thoughtless people have done. If you don't have permission to hike on someone else's property, stay out.

Be polite

Step off the trail to allow faster hikers, horses, and people traveling in the opposite direction to pass safely.

Take only pictures, leave only footprints, and kill only time

In other words, try to make as little impact as possible in the area where you hike.

* * *

My mother always says, "If you tell the truth, later on you won't have to worry about what you said." We can say the same about behavior: if we do the right thing, we won't have to worry about what we've done. In both instances, the reward is a clear conscience.

DEALING WITH THE UNMENTIONABLE

When Mom Nature calls, find a private spot off the trail. If you are near a stream, pond, or lake, try to stay at least 100 feet above the high water mark—that bathtub ring of debris left by spring runoff—in an area free of poison ivy, oak, or sumac; stinging nettles; or sleeping animals.

If "Number One" is the focus, boys and men can unzip and let 'er rip. The distaff set, however, needs a bit more preparation.

Since squatting invariably leads to wet socks (at the very least), I have developed a sure-fire method for helping little

When Mother Nature calls, find a private spot off the trail.

girls whiz in the woods: 1) Pull her pants down around her ankles. 2) With her back to your chest, clasp your hands under her knees as she loops her arms over yours, and pick her up. 3) Position her bare bottom directly over her target. Now she can relax and do her duty, securely cradled by her parent. Even a toddler midway through toilet training delights in this new form of togetherness. In fact, "going potty" became a social event for each of my daughters and me.

Bigger girls or women can keep their feet high and dry by using a similar, but unassisted, method recommended by Kathleen Meyer, author of *How to Shit in the Woods*. Meyer suggests finding two large rocks or logs that are close together. Lower your pants around your ankles, ease back against one rock or log, and put your feet up on the other. Relax and fire away.

Both sexes can use either of these techniques for defecation.

Speaking of "Number Two," if you are not hiking in a pack in/pack out area, bury your excrement in a 6- to 8-inch-deep hole. You can dig your hole before or after you've finished your business, but the hole, its contents, and their subsequent burial, are absolutely necessary to speed decay and to eliminate an unsightly mess for other hikers. For this chore, you need a plastic hiker's trowel and a resealable plastic bag to pack out used toilet paper, sanitary supplies, or "disposable" diapers if you are changing an infant. Dispose of your infant's poop as you would your own.

If you find you left the TP at home, try wiping with

large, soft leaves. Don't strip one plant, but take your time and gather what you need from several. And make sure that whatever you use is not poisonous or prickly. In areas that prohibit picking plants, try using a smooth, sun-baked stone that is cool to the touch.

To really clean up after yourself or your little darling, bring along some wipes (toss used ones in your resealable bag), or haul water in two containers at least 100 feet from a lake or stream. Squirt some biodegradable soap in the first container to wash yourself, your child, clothing, or whatever, then rinse with water from the second container and empty both containers before returning to the trail.

5

Family Backpacking:
Take It to the Limit

I washed my hands in water
That never rained nor run;
I dried them with a towel
That was never wove nor spun.
What did I use?
(dew and sun)

Once your family is seasoned and hiking its umpteenth trail, someone (maybe even you) will blurt out, "This spot is so pretty, I wish we could camp right here!" If you see nods all around, it might be time to take hiking to a new level—backpacking.

Make sure the entire family understands that backpacking means carrying your food, clothing, and shelter on your back. No fast-food joints or convenience stores await your business several miles from the trailhead. Each backpacker in the family is responsible for sharing the load, as well as the planning.

And here is where I separate the babies from the capable children.

Yes, some parents do take their infants and toddlers backpacking—they are probably the ones who also enjoy breech deliveries after 36 hours of labor with no anesthetics. Backpacking with very young children means that one parent carries the baby, clean diapers, dirty diapers (pack in/pack out), infant clothing, infant toys, and the rest of baby's needs, while the other parent (or miscellaneous adult) carries the tent, the food, the cooking equipment, the sleeping bags, personal gear for both adults, plus everything else. Ask yourself, is it worth carrying 60 pounds or more so that you can sleep on the forest floor with an infant who needs multiple diaper changes in the middle of the night and won't remember the trip anyway?

My recommendation: Stick to day hikes until your youngsters can walk briskly down the trail with a fair portion of the load. If you insist on backpacking, leave the babies at home. Make backpacking a rite of passage to celebrate growing capabilities, not an ordeal.

I took each of my children backpacking the summer after their fourth birthdays. We accompanied other families with older kids who served as role models for my preschoolers and shared their communal tents. My four-year-old of the moment carried his/her clothing, while I hauled my personal gear, one roomy sleeping bag to share, and food and kitchen equipment for two.

Even when youngsters are old enough to haul their own sleeping bags and clothing, family backpacking depends on how much parents are willing to carry. One dad describes the participants of his first family backpacking trips as "Mom, the kid, and the mule."

A loaded backpack should weigh no more than one-fourth of a person's weight. Every hiker, however, no matter what age, weight, or stature, has a personal pack-weight threshold. Weight at or under that threshold allows hiking in reasonable comfort. Beyond the threshold, backpacking becomes grueling. The best way to find your personal weight limit is through trial and error on short hikes, keeping in mind that distance, terrain, and weather all make additional demands on energy and stamina.

Follow the K.I.S.S. principle (Keep It Simple, Silly) when loading your backpack. Think about the rooms in your house and what they provide. A sleeping bag, pad, tent, and rain-fly create a bedroom and living room. A camp stove, fuel, a large pot, food, and one cup and one spoon per person (no need for a full place setting), provide an outdoor kitchen. Bring along the contents of your daypack, which already includes items for your bathroom (including the medicine chest) and closet. Add a washcloth and small towel, toothbrush and toothpaste, extra underwear and socks, an extra shirt or two, a second pair of shoes to use as camp or water shoes, and you are set. Supplies for a typical two to three day backpacking trip are listed in Appendix III.

Organize your pack so that you can easily find what you need. Put your water bottle, lunch, and rainwear in outside pockets or at the top of the main compartment where you can reach them without digging.

Load the heaviest stuff toward the top and front of your pack, where it will rest against your back and shoulders and balance your load vertically. Carried to extremes, a top-heavy pack will be tipsy, so use common sense. Adjust and re-adjust the shoulder straps and hip belt to find your comfort zone.

Don't be too ambitious on your first overnight hike. Hike a mile or two, then find a level spot to pitch your tent where there is good drainage, shelter from the wind and sun, and no nearby anthills or poisonous plants.

Food attracts bears and other animals, so stow yours properly. For safety's sake, don't eat or store food (*any* food, including wrapped candy—this includes toiletries and any-thing that *smells* like food) in your tent. Pitch your tent at least 30 feet away from your camp kitchen. Find a stout tree to hang food and anything scented at least 10 feet above the ground and 5 feet away from the trunk. When food is left where bears can reach it, people and bears are both at risk.

In most public forests, parks, and recreation areas, bears that raid campsites are removed from the area, if possible. If they become repeat offenders and a perceived threat to hu-mans, they are destroyed. Please care for your food properly and don't cause problems for a bear.

When your family is ready to try backpacking for more than one night, you may want to pitch your tent just once and limit yourselves to day hikes from this base camp. If you decide to change locations, get an early start so that you arrive at your new campsite with plenty of time to set up, explore, and relax. A late start means less time to enjoy the new camp before sundown and probably disappointed campers.

Enjoying a night together under the stars.

Backpacking beyond civilization means reconnecting to natural rhythms. Without the benefit of artificial light, you crawl into your sleeping bags when the sun goes down, and emerge with the morning sun.

Some children have no trouble sleeping in a dark tent, while others panic if they awaken in total darkness. Keep a flashlight handy for a night light. Some people may find tent walls confining. If that is the case, keep a window or door open, but make sure the mosquito netting is in place! The littlest backpacker may be most content snuggling with a parent in one sleeping bag. Sharing a sleeping bag has its advantages (like saving weight) but, for me, a good night's sleep was never one of them.

However you handle your sleeping arrangements, make sure your kids get the full camp experience—setting up camp, hauling water, gathering firewood (if open fires are permitted), and cooking meals. Backpacking bonds the whole family when everyone pitches in.

"When there is no milk delivery and what you have is on your back, you have to depend upon each other," according to the matriarch of one family of dedicated backpackers.

BACKPACKING BUYS

In the last decade of the twentieth century, outdoor gear manufacturers finally discovered children. The quality and availability of children's outdoor gear continue to improve.

Backpacks

Backpacks "just like Mom's and Dad's" that grow with your child feature telescoping, anatomically correct suspension systems that adjust to fit torsos between 12" and 21" long. Well-padded shoulder straps and hip belts help protect developing bones and muscles. Rugged ripstop nylon packcloth stands up to abuse.

Adult backpacks come with internal or external frames and a host of options. Check out your local outdoor store or catalog for the latest styles and gee-gaws.

Sleeping bags

Lightweight mummy bags are available to fit kids up to 5 feet tall. Mummy bags are shaped like cocoons, roomier in the upper body, tapering gradually toward the bottom for warmth and comfort. They feature contoured hoods to maximize warmth and coziness, and some include zip-on extensions to grow with their users. Synthetic insulation (which makes bags more easily washable) provides comfort ratings of 15 to 30 degrees F. Special stuff sacks compress sleeping bags for kids or adults into packages about the size of a loaf of bread. Lightweight sleeping bags weigh 2 lb. 13 oz.–3 lb. 6 oz.

Tents

A two-person tent is too small for three, while a three-person tent is just right for two adults and a small child. Shop for a tent that is lightweight and easy to assemble.

ZERO IMPACT

Besides abiding by the trail etiquette for day hikers discussed on pages 42–49, backpackers have an additional responsibility to leave zero impact when they camp.

- Find a campsite away from the trail and the bank of any stream, pond, or lake.
- Choose a spot that doesn't need to be dug up or leveled for your comfort.
- Haul, use, and dump water away from your camp and at least 100 feet from its source. Use only biodegradable, non-phosphate soap to clean dishes and for personal hygiene.

- Pack in/pack out garbage and, if the area requires it, human waste. When the rules allow disposal, bury scrapings from dishes and pots and human waste according to the procedures described on pages 48–49.
- Where campfires are permitted, use an old fire ring if one is available. If a new ring is needed, dig a shallow fire pit and set aside the topsoil and vegetation to reclaim the site after use. Clear away natural flammables, use dry, fallen wood, and keep your fire small.
- When you break camp, pick up all litter from the fire pit and around camp (whether or not it is yours), scatter extra firewood and rocks from the fire ring, and use a fallen bough or stick to erase signs of your presence as much as possible.

6

Hiking's Legacy:
Passing On
Environmental Values

Red and blue and delicate green;
The king can't catch it and neither can the queen.
Pull it in the room and you can catch it soon.
Answer this riddle by tomorrow at noon.
(rainbow)

As a young boy, Meriwether Lewis loved to ramble into the
mountains near his home in Albemarle County, Virginia,
immersing himself in the habitats of native flora and fauna.
As a teenager, Lewis hiked farther still—all the way to
Georgia, where he continued to study and explore. His
insatiable curiosity, self-reliance, and ability to walk long distances caught the eye of Thomas Jefferson, who later offered
Lewis a job and a solid place in history as the leader of the
Lewis and Clark Expedition.

Meticulous field notes in the expedition journals reflect
Lewis's love of nature. Such careful recording is not without
precedent, however. Around 850 B.C., Homer became the
world's first known nature writer when his observations cre-
ated the backdrop for *The Iliad* and *The Odyssey*. Five hundred
years later, Aristotle authored several works on natural sci-

ence. Five hundred years after Aristotle, the Bible included psalms celebrating the wonders of nature and stories of how Jesus and others retreated to the wilderness to unwind and reflect. Oral histories tell us that, throughout time, native peoples embraced the earth's rhythms and sought visions in sacred wild places.

In the western world, hiking and the study of natural sciences became popular pastimes as the industrial revolution introduced leisure time. In the mid-nineteenth century, writers like Henry David Thoreau reached a broad and eager audience with their essays on the virtues of nature, setting the stage for future preservation movements.

One of the first such movements in the U.S. identified threats to the natural bounty and oddities of a remote western region, culminating in 1872 with the establishment of the world's first national park. The creation of Yellowstone National Park generated a flurry of preservation victories throughout the twentieth century, as Congress set aside still more national parks, wilderness areas, wild and scenic rivers, wildlife refuges, and natural areas.

Because of the wisdom and the continued work of modern conservationists, we still can embrace our inheritance and experience nature anew. That experience, however, comes with a price. America's wildlands are preserved through the democratic process, and their future, as well as the future of other deserving lands, depends on our vigilance and the wise decision-making of our leaders.

What can families do to make sure wildlands are

preserved for another millennium?

- Find out about what is happening where you live and in the places where you hike.
- Participate in the activities of a local nature center, or through membership organizations like Boy Scouts or Girl Scouts. Kids also can start their own nature clubs, or affiliate with larger child-centered organizations.
- Join a local, state, or national organization that works to keep things wild. Contribute what you can and add your voice to a democratic discussion about issues of concern.

* * *

Ownership and empowerment lead to change and wise stewardship. So introduce your children to their inheritance by taking them hiking and sharing the responsibility of stewardship. Citizenship comes with rights *and* responsibilities. It is up to all of us to ensure that the lands through which we ramble remain intact, and that other wild places receive the protection they deserve.

Appreciation and wonder are as old as time itself. Nurture them in yourselves and in your children, and pass them along with the knowledge that each generation is responsible for what it leaves for the next.

First-Aid and Emergency Kits

Items in both the first-aid kit and the emergency kit can be distributed among adults on a family hike. Each adult is responsible for knowing how to use the contents of each kit and should know where they are stowed.

FIRST-AID KIT

- ☐ Antibiotic ointment
- ☐ Antiseptic
- ☐ Bandaging materials (2" adhesive tape, gauze roll, adhesive bandages, butterfly bandages, 3" x 3" sterile dressings, 3" elastic wrap)
- ☐ Tweezers, scissors, and safety pins
- ☐ Ibuprofen, aspirin, and children's acetaminophen
- ☐ Prescription painkiller
- ☐ Antihistamine
- ☐ Moleskin (to prevent or treat blisters)
- ☐ Snakebite kit

EMERGENCY KIT

☐ 9' x 12' Plastic tarp (for an emergency shelter)

☐ Nylon cord (at least 50 feet to bind poles for an emergency shelter or to tie a splint in place)

☐ Matches and commercial firestarter in a waterproof container (may also include waterproof matches, disposable butane lighter, and candle)

☐ Signal mirror

☐ Fluorescent plastic flagging

☐ Large plastic garbage bags

☐ Money ($20, plus coins for telephone). Recommand a calling card. Sometimes a pay phone demands more change than you brought.

Daypack Essentials and Extras

Every hiker needs to know when and how to use the contents of his/her daypack.

PERSONAL EMERGENCY EQUIPMENT

- ☐ Emergency whistle (to signal for help)
- ☐ Small flashlight with extra batteries and bulb (reverse one battery so the flashlight can't switch on accidentally)
- ☐ Pocket-sized space blanket
- ☐ Extra personal prescription medication (in case of delay)
- ☐ Allergy medication (including bee sting kit, if sensitive)
- ☐ "Sacred" high-energy candy bar
- ☐ Personal identification
- ☐ Pencil and small notebook
- ☐ Car keys (each adult should carry a set)
- ☐ Pepper spray (if hiking in bear country)

PERSONAL ESSENTIALS

- ☐ Rainwear or big garbage bag for substitute
- ☐ Sweatshirt (preferably polar fleece)

- ☐ Extra pair of socks
- ☐ 1 liter or more of water
- ☐ Lemon drops
- ☐ Bandanna (to use as sunshade, ear muffs, washcloth, towel, sling)
- ☐ Sunglasses
- ☐ Plastic bags for litter
- ☐ Common sense, a sense of humor, and a positive attitude

FAMILY ESSENTIALS TO DISTRIBUTE AMONG ADULTS

- ☐ Map
- ☐ Compass
- ☐ Pocket knife with variety of blades
- ☐ Water purification system or iodine tablets
- ☐ Trail food
- ☐ Insect repellent
- ☐ Sunscreen (for lips, face, and body)
- ☐ Toilet paper and plastic trowel (for bathroom needs)
- ☐ Wire or duct tape (because you never know)

EXTRAS TO MAKE HIKING EVEN MORE FUN

- ☐ Folding umbrella
- ☐ Telescopic hiking poles
- ☐ Camera with accessories and extra film (include a single-use waterproof camera for each older child)
- ☐ Binoculars and/or spotting scope
- ☐ Plant and animal fieldguides

- ☐ Science kit (plastic bug jar or similar container to catch and release creepy crawlies—empty grated cheese containers or spice jars with perforated lids work well; tweezers; magnifying glass)
- ☐ Flower press (if flower-picking is permissible)
- ☐ Writing and drawing supplies (sketchbooks or journals; pens and pencils, watercolors)
- ☐ Fishing gear (including licenses and local regulations)

ITEMS TO LEAVE IN THE CAR

You don't have to take everything-but-the-kitchen-sink each time you hike. Use your good common sense. If you know you won't get more than a mile down the trail, just take the bare minimum and leave the bulk of emergency supplies and essentials in your car. When you start hiking greater distances, some things still can be stowed, like extra food, water, blankets, clothing, a second first aid-kit, a large flashlight, and negative vibes.

Backpacking Essentials

Carry everything listed in Appendixes I and II, plus the following:

FIRST-AID KIT

☐ Antacids, laxatives, and anti-diarrheal medication

PERSONAL ESSENTIALS

☐ Sleeping bag and pad
☐ Extra shirts, underwear, and socks
☐ Extra shoes to use as camp or water shoes
☐ Wash cloth and small towel
☐ Toothbrush and toothpaste
☐ Cup and spoon
☐ Extra pair of prescription eyeglasses
☐ Knee brace (if you are prone to sore knees)

FAMILY ESSENTIALS TO DISTRIBUTE AMONG ADULTS

☐ Tent and rainfly
☐ Food

- ☐ Camp stove and leak-proof fuel bottle
- ☐ Cooking pots (at least two to haul water for washing people and dishes) and cooking utensils
- ☐ Biodegradable soap, dish rag, and dish towel
- ☐ Extra boot laces
- ☐ Needle and thread
- ☐ Bungee cords
- ☐ Folding saw, ring saw, or hatchet (use only to build an emergency shelter or cut up dried and fallen wood for a fire)
- ☐ Sharpening stone
- ☐ Candle lantern (optional)

APPENDIX IV

Trail Food

Food is an important part of any family hike, so pack a surplus of goodies that can withstand being stuffed into a daypack without refrigeration.

When sandwiches are on the menu, choose fixings that don't require special treatment. Use meats and cheeses only if you plan to eat lunch within a reasonable time. Individually packaged condiments can be added on the trail to make sandwiches taste "just made." Peanut butter and jelly are usually popular, no matter when or where they are served.

Pita bread, English muffins, or soft tortillas can substitute for sandwich bread, which is inevitably smashed flat in a daypack. To avoid complaints about a soggy repast, pack tortillas and sandwich fixings separately and assemble on the trail.

Easy-to-pack snacks include carrots, apples, dried fruit, nuts, pretzels, and individually wrapped string cheeses. Leave crumbly cookies and crackers and squishy fruits, like bananas and apricots, at home unless you are willing to dedicate valuable space in your daypack to bulky protective packaging. Even swathed in tissue paper and bubble wrap, such edibles might not survive to lunchtime.

Recipes for a few trail favorites appear in the following text.

G.O.R.P. (GOOD OL' RAISINS AND PEANUTS)

Mix and bag 1 cup raisins and 1 cup dry roasted peanuts with 1 cup each of one or more of the following: roasted sunflower seeds, roasted soybeans, chopped dried apples or apricots, carob chips, coated chocolate candies.

TRAIL MIX

Mix and bag 2 cups dried cereal (not flakes), 2 cups small cheese crackers, 1 cup nuts, 1 cup small pretzels, 1 cup raisins, 1/4 cup shelled sunflower, pumpkin, or sesame seeds.

ENERGY BARS

In a medium-sized bowl, combine 3/4 cup peanut butter, 1/2 cup honey and 1 teaspoon vanilla; blend thoroughly. In a separate bowl, mix together 3/4 cup skim milk powder and 1 cup oatmeal. Gradually add milk mixture plus 1/4 cup toasted sesame seeds to the peanut butter mixture. Add 2 tablespoons boiled water and blend well. Shape mixture into 1" by 2" bars and roll the bars in more sesame seeds. Wrap bars individually and refrigerate overnight so they solidify.

CARDAMOM BARS

Melt together 1 cup honey and 3 tablespoons margarine. In a separate bowl, stir together 2 cups whole wheat flour,

1 tablespoon baking powder, 2 teaspoons cinnamon, 1/2 teaspoon cardamom, and 1/4 teaspoon ground cloves. Add flour mixture plus 1/2 cup sunflower seeds or chopped walnuts and 1/4 cup each grated orange peel and grated lemon peel to the honey mixture. Pat into a greased 9" x 13" pan. Bake 20-25 minutes at 350 degrees F. Cool and cut into bars. Store in an airtight container; package individual bars in plastic wrap for the trail.

About the Author

A journalism graduate of the University of Montana, Robin also is the author of *Young People's Guide to Yellowstone National Park* (Stoneydale Press, 1985) and *Family Fun in Yellowstone* (Falcon Publishing, 1998). She has written about conservation for publications such as *Living Wilderness, Montana Magazine, High Country News,* the *Denver Post,* and *Western Wildlands.* Committed to conservation stewardship and education, Robin serves on the boards of the Cinnabar Foundation and the Montana Natural History Center. In 1976 Robin and her late husband Philip received the American Motors Conservation Award for their conservation work.

Robin lives in a forested canyon on the outskirts of Missoula, Montana, with her husband William Nichols, daughter Whitney, one dog, two horses, two llamas, and an occasional pet spider.

get
FALCON GUIDED

SCENIC DRIVING GUIDES

Scenic Driving Alaska and the Yukon
Scenic Driving Arizona
Scenic Driving the Beartooth Highway
Scenic Driving British Columbia
Scenic Driving California
Scenic Driving Colorado
Scenic Driving Florida
Scenic Driving Georgia
Scenic Driving Hawaii
Scenic Driving Idaho
Scenic Driving Kentucky
Scenic Driving Michigan
Scenic Driving Minnesota
Scenic Driving Montana
Scenic Driving New England
Scenic Driving New Mexico
Scenic Driving North Carolina
Scenic Driving Oregon

Scenic Driving the Ozarks including
    the Ouchita Mountains
Scenic Driving Pennsylvania
Scenic Driving Texas
Scenic Driving Utah
Scenic Driving Virginia
Scenic Driving Washington
Scenic Driving Wisconsin
Scenic Driving Wyoming
Scenic Driving Yellowstone and
    Grand Teton National Parks

National Forest Scenic Byways:
    East & South
National Forest Scenic Byways:
    Far West
National Forest Scenic Byways:
    Rocky Mountains

**To order check with your local bookseller
or call Falcon at 1-800-582-2665.
www.Falcon.com**

FALCON®

get FALCON GUIDED

BIRDING GUIDES

Birding Georgia
Birding Illinois
Birding Minnesota
Birding Montana
Birding Northern California
Birding Texas
Birding Utah

America's 100 Most Wanted Birds
Birder's Dictionary

FISHING GUIDES

Fishing Alaska
Fishing the Beartooths
Fishing Florida
Fishing Glacier National Park
Fishing Maine
Fishing Montana
Fishing Wyoming
Fishing Yellowstone National Park

America's 100 Best Trout Streams
America's 50 Best Bass Waters

To order check with your local bookseller
or call Falcon at 1-800-582-2665.
www.Falcon.com

FALCON®

get
FALCON GUIDED

Field Guides

Bitterroot: Montana State Flower
Canyon Country Wildflowers
Central Rocky Mountain Wildflowers
Chihuahuan Desert Wildflowers
Great Lakes Berry Book
New England Berry Book
Ozark Wildflowers
Pacific Northwest Berry Book
Plants of Arizona
Rare Plants of Colorado
Rocky Mountain Berry Book
Scats & Tracks of the Pacific Coast
Scats & Tracks of the Rocky Mountains
Sierra Nevada Wildflowers
Southern Rocky Mountain Wildflowers
Tallgrass Prairie Wildflowers
Western Trees

To order check with your local bookseller
or call Falcon at 1-800-582-2665.
www.Falcon.com

FALCONGUIDES ®Leading the Way™

FalconGuides® are available for where-to-go hiking, mountain biking, rock climbing, walking, scenic driving, fishing, rockhounding, paddling, birding, wildlife viewing, and camping. We also have FalconGuides on essential outdoor skills and subjects and field identification. The following titles are currently available, but this list grows every year.

For a free catalog with a complete list of titles, call FALCON toll-free at 1-800-582-2665.

BEST EASY DAY HIKES SERIES

To order any of these books, check with your local bookseller or call FALCON ® at 1-800-582-2665.
Visit us on the world wide web at:
www.Falcon.com

FALCON®

FALCONGUIDES ®Leading the Way™

Published in cooperation with Defenders of Wildlife, the Watchable Wildlife® Series is the official series of guidebooks for the National Watchable Wildlife Program. This highly successful program is a unique partnership of state and federal agencies and a private organization. Each full-color guidebook in the Watchable Wildlife® series features detailed site descriptions, side trips, viewing tips, and easy-to-follow maps.

WILDLIFE VIEWING GUIDES

Alaska Wildlife Viewing Guide

Arizona Wildlife Viewing Guide

California Wildlife Viewing Guide

Colorado Wildlife Viewing Guide

Florida Wildlife Viewing Guide

Indiana Wildlife Vewing Guide

Iowa Wildlife Viewing Guide

Kentucky Wildlife Viewing Guide

Massachusetts Wildlife Viewing Guide

Montana Wildlife Viewing Guide

Nebraska Wildlife Viewing Guide

Nevada Wildlife Viewing Guide

New Hampshire Wildlife Viewing Guide

New Jersey Wildlife Viewing Guide

New Mexico Wildlife Viewing Guide

New York Wildlife Viewing Guide

North Carolina Wildlife Viewing Guide

North Dakota Wildlife Viewing Guide

Ohio Wildlife Viewing Guide

Oregon Wildlife Viewing Guide

Puerto Rico & the Virgin Islands Wildlife Viewing Guide

Tennessee Wildlife Viewing Guide

Texas Wildlife Viewing Guide

Utah Wildlife Viewing Guide

Vermont Wildlife Viewing Guide

Virginia Wildlife Viewing Guide

Washington Wildlife Viewing Guide

West Virginia Wildife Viewing Guide

Wisconsin Wildlife Viewing Guide

To order any of these books, check with your local bookseller or call Falcon® at
1-800-582-2665.
www.Falcon.com

FALCON®

Hiking

Best Hikes Along the Continental
   Divide
Hiking Alaska
Hiking Arizona
Hiking Arizona's Cactus Country
Hiking the Beartooths
Hiking Big Bend National Park
Hiking the BobMarshall Country
Hiking California
Hiking California's Desert Parks
Hiking Carlsbad/Guadalupe
Hiking Colorado
Hiking Colorado, Vol.II
Hiking Colorado's Summits
Hiking Colorado's Weminuche
   Wilderness
Hiking the ColumbiaRiver Gorge
Hiking Florida
Hiking Georgia
Hiking Glacier/Waterton Lakes
Hiking Grand Canyon
Hiking Grand Staircase-Escalante
Hiking Grand TetonNational Park
Hiking Great Basin Nat'l Park
Hiking Hot Springs in the Pacific
   Northwest
Hiking Idaho
Hiking Maine
Hiking Maryland and Delaware
Hiking Michigan
Hiking Minnesota
Hiking Montana
Hiking Mount RainierNational Park
Hiking Mount St. Helens
Hiking Nevada
Hiking New Hampshire
Hiking New Mexico
Hiking New Mexico's Gila Wilderness
Hiking New York

Hiking North Carolina
Hiking the North Cascades
Hiking Northern Arizona
Hiking Northern California
Hiking Olympic National Park
Hiking Oregon
Hiking Oregon's Central Cascades
Hiking Oregon's Eagle Cap
Hiking Oregon's Mt. Hood
Hiking Oregon's Three Sisters
Hiking Pennsylvania
Hiking Ruins Seldom Seen
Hiking Shenandoah
Hiking the Sierra Nevada
Hiking South Carolina
Hiking South Dakota's BlackHills
   Country
Hiking Southern New England
Hiking Tennessee
Hiking Texas
Hiking Utah
Hiking Utah's Summits
Hiking Vermont
Hiking Virginia
Hiking Washington
Hiking Wyoming
Hiking Wyoming's CloudPeak
   Wilderness
Hiking Wyoming's Teton
   andWashakie Wilderness
Hiking Wyoming's WindRiver
   Range
Hiking YellowstoneNational Park
Hiking Yosemite
Hiking Zion & Bryce Canyon
Exploring Canyonlands & Arches
Wild Country Companion
Wild Montana
Wild Utah